HOME RUN
Kings

Jeff
Savage

RSVP

RAINTREE
STECK-VAUGHN
PUBLISHERS
A Steck-Vaughn Company

Austin, Texas

Published by
Raintree Steck–Vaughn Publishers, an imprint of Steck–Vaughn Company

Library of Congress Cataloging-in-Publication Data
Savage, Jeff, 1961-
    Home run kings / by Jeff Savage.
        p.   cm.
    Includes index.
    Summary: Surveys the history of the home run in baseball, concentrating
on famous home run hitters and the ongoing race to beat the previous home
run record.
    ISBN 0-7398-0216-X   (hardcover)
    ISBN 0-7398-0215-1   (softcover)
    1. Home runs (Baseball) — United States — History — Juvenile literature.
2. Baseball players — Rating of — United States — Juvenile literature.
3. Baseball — Records — United States — Juvenile literature.   [1. Home runs
(Baseball)   2. Baseball — History.   3. Baseball players.]   I. Title.
GV868.4.S38   1999
796.357'26 — dc21   98-56021
                                                                                  CIP
                                                                                  AC

Printed in the United States of America
10 9 8 7 6 5 4 3 2 1 LB 02 01 00 99
Project Management, Design & Electronic Production: Gino Coverty
Cover Design: Gino Coverty

Photo Acknowledgments
Cover: (McGwire) ©Stephen Dunn/Allsport; (Sosa) ©Brian Bahr/Allsport; (Babe Ruth)
©Hulton Deutsch/Allsport; (Maris) ©Photo File.

National Baseball Hall of Fame Library, Cooperstown, NY: pages 4, 9, 10, 14, 22, 37, 38, 39,40, 41,
42, 45; Brian Spurlock: page 6; AP Wide World Photos: page 17; Carl Kidwiler: page 20; St. Louis
Baseball Cardinals (Dan Donovan) photo: pages 24, 27, 29; Stephen Green Photography: pages
31, 32, 34.

Contents

Boston's famed Fenway Park, scene of many of baseball's home runs.

Big Sticks

aseball is a quiet game interrupted by moments of flurry and joy. Watching a no-hitter unfold is a fidget, a play at the plate a thrill, a stolen base a rush, a great catch a stir. A home run is something different and something more. Of all the plays of the game, it is the home run that excites America's fans most. We love hearing the crack of the bat. Our breath is taken away at that precise instant when we think Could it be? We love seeing the ball soar until it becomes a tiny pea and disappears over the wall. We love to celebrate as our hero dances happily around the bases. We love feeling the drama and emotion of the home run.

Maybe a home run is such a treat because it is so hard to accomplish. At 60 feet, 6 inches from the pitching rubber to home plate, a typical 85-mile-per-hour pitch gets from the pitcher's hand to the catcher's mitt in less than half a second.

**Mark McGwire was crowned king
with his 70th homer.**

Half a second. That's all the time a batter has to see the pitch, decide to swing at it, and make perfect contact. It seems nearly impossible.

An African proverb made popular by President Theodore Roosevelt goes, "Speak softly and carry a big stick; you will go far." Roosevelt could have been talking about baseball. A major league baseball bat weighs about two pounds and measures less than three inches in diameter, yet it seems much larger in the mighty hands of the home run hitter. Mark McGwire and Sammy Sosa made history in the summer of 1998 when they bashed record-breaking home runs. Others had come before. Babe Ruth gained such fame with his wallops in the 1920s that the longest of balls hit by others were described as "Ruthian." Roger Maris rocked the baseball world in 1961 when he broke The Babe's seemingly unbreakable single-season record. There were more. Hank Aaron became the all-time home run leader, with Willie Mays and Frank Robinson, Harmon Killebrew and Reggie Jackson, Mike Schmidt and Mickey Mantle not far behind.

Today it is Ken Griffey, Jr. and Barry Bonds and others who electrify the crowds with their mammoth blasts. Pitchers, fielders, and baserunners are admired for their skills. But power hitters are the players most revered. These are the players who walk softly and carry a big stick and go far with the ball.

These are the home run kings.

The Babe

*H*ome runs were a rare sight in baseball's early years. From the birth of the National League in 1876 to the arrival of the American League in 1901, and for another 15 years afterward, pitchers dominated the sport because the rules were in their favor. They could "doctor" the ball by spitting licorice or tobacco juice on it or scuffing it with sandpaper or cleats. And no matter how mangled the ball got, the umpire never threw it out of play. This was known as the dead ball era.

Then came Babe Ruth. His monstrous power changed the game. It helped that spitters were eventually outlawed, and that livelier balls were made by baseball manufacturers, but it was Ruth alone who introduced home run excitement to baseball. The biggest power hitter to that point was Frank "Home Run" Baker, who led the league four straight years

Something The Babe enjoyed as much as swatting home runs was watching them soar out of the park.

The Babe spent much of his time
choosing the right bat.

with totals of 11, 10, 12, and 9. Six years later, in 1920, Ruth had arrived and was swinging away. He clouted 54 homers that season, more than every other American League team.

Ruth wasn't always a home run hitter. George Herman Ruth had spent most of his childhood in a reform school for boys in Baltimore, Maryland, where he learned the rudiments of pitching. In 1914 he joined the Boston Red Sox as a pitcher, and soon he was the ace of the league, leading the Sox to three World Series. There he set a scoreless-innings record that would last for 40 years. In his first full season with the Sox he hit only four homers.

In 1919 the New York Yankees acquired Ruth from the Red Sox and convinced him to quit pitching and concentrate on hitting. That year he clubbed 29 homers to break the major league record. When he nearly doubled that total the next season he was bestowed with such nicknames as the "Sultan of Swat," the "Bambino," and, simply, "The Babe." Yankee Stadium, which opened upon Ruth's arrival, became known as "The House That Ruth Built."

By this time stories of Ruth's enormous appetite and pictures of his bowling ball body were appearing in newspapers across the country. For breakfast he might consume a huge steak, half a dozen eggs, half a loaf of bread, and a pot of coffee. His favorite meal after games was a quart of chocolate ice cream and pickled eels. When Ruth and his Yankees pulled into train stations it was like the circus had arrived. Fans filled stadiums to see The Babe drag his bat to the plate, dig his feet in the box, take that long stride forward, and wallop one out.

The 1927 Yankees featured a fierce slugging lineup known as "Murderer's Row," and in the middle of it was The Babe. Though Ruth never admitted it, he seemed bothered early that season by the attention given to an emerging young star named Lou Gehrig. Babe recaptured the spotlight by making it known he intended to break the record for homers in a season. Whose record would he break? His own, of course. Six years earlier he had hit 59.

Ruth swung for the fences like never before, and with each home run blast he put a notch in his bat, until the bat split

12

after the 21st notch. He was left with three favorite bats—Black Betsy, Beautiful Bella, and Big Bertha. Reporters wrote such dramatic accounts that it was hard to separate fact from fiction. It was reported in the May 31 editions of the *New York Times* that "The Babe hit a baseball so hard in practice that he broke it in two." Ruth's fame was matched that year only by Charles Lindbergh, who became a national hero by flying an airplane nonstop from New York to Paris.

Crowds roared their cheers for Ruth each trip he took around the bases, and The Babe soaked it up, tipping his cap and waving to his fans. Moments after he hit number 54, a 10-year-old boy jumped onto the field at Yankee Stadium and handed him the ball and a pen asking for his autograph. The Babe signed it. Upon clouting number 56 he carried his bat around the bases with him, and when a boy ran onto the field and grabbed hold of the bat, Ruth dragged him with the bat across home plate and into the dugout. He hit number 59 with Black Betsy to tie his own mark, then blasted number 60 with Beautiful Bella. "Sixty!"

Team:
New York Yankees

Player #:
3

Lifetime Batting Average:
.342

# of HRs (1927):
60

Lefty / Righty:
Left

Positions Played:
Pitcher, Left Field

Ruth

he bellowed in the clubhouse, according to newspaper reports. "Count 'em. Sixty!"

Ruth's 15th and last homer of his World Series career was the famed "called shot" in which he pointed to the bleachers to signal where he was going to deposit the next pitch and then did so with a tremendous clout. He hit the last homer of his great career, number 714, over the roof of Pittsburgh's Forbes Field. It was the first ball ever to clear the roof and it landed in a construction site where a boy retrieved it and brought it to Ruth. The Babe signed it and gave it back to the boy.

Roger Maris

As much as Babe Ruth was revered for setting his home run record, the man who broke his mark was reviled for it. Roger Maris never wanted to be the new Babe Ruth, and he said so over and over again. Yet in the amazing season of 1961, Maris was one home run better than Ruth.

Roger learned to hit the baseball between the snowbanks of the upper Midwest, first in Hibbing, Minnesota, and then, after age 11, in Fargo, North Dakota. He was signed as an outfielder at age 18 by the Cleveland Indians organization and he reached the majors four years later in 1957. After a season with the Indians he was traded to Kansas City where he played two years with the Royals. He hit 58 home runs total those first three seasons, and so no one mistook him for a home run king. But he was a lefty pull-hitter with a smooth, level swing, and Yankee Stadium had a short porch

Maris spent most of his career under the strain of beating Ruth's home run record.

in right, and so the Yanks traded four players to bring him to New York to see what he could do. Maris belted 39 home runs his first season in the Bronx, and he edged out teammate Mickey Mantle to win the league Most Valuable Player award. That's when the trouble started.

Mantle was a 10-year veteran and the best switch-hitter ever, a glamour boy, and the most popular player in the game. No one beat Mickey Mantle out of anything. Who did this Midwestern kid named Maris think he was, anyway? The truth is, while passionate New Yorkers voiced their opinions, and the newspapers played it up as a duel, Roger and Mickey were friends. They were even roommates on the road. So it proved fitting that a year later, in that fateful season of 1961, they would duel as friends for the home run record.

Mantle opened the '61 season with a bang. By the time Maris hit his fourth home run, Mantle already had 10. But Roger's bat heated up, and six weeks later when summer arrived, Maris clubbed his 24th homer to overtake his friend. With both Yankees sluggers reaching 30 a month later, and the

New York papers running a daily chart comparing their pace to the immortal Babe's, baseball commissioner Ford Frick did a strange and awful thing. Frick ordered that "a distinguishing mark" be placed next to the man's name in the official base-ball record book if he broke Ruth's record after 154 games. That's how long the seasons were when Ruth played. Baseball seasons had been expanded eight games since then to 162. But conditions in baseball had changed in many other ways in the three decades since the legendary Ruth played, such as new teams, new ballparks, and the introduction of night games. Also, Frick deemed that any other record to be broken after 154 games would not require a distinguishing mark, only this one. The real reason Frick cast his silly order was because he was a ghostwriter and friend of Ruth's, penning poems and stories that The Babe took credit for.

The more Maris continued to bang out bombs, stretching his total farther ahead of Mantle's and within reach of the record, the more nervous he grew. He abused his body by drinking jugs of black coffee and smoking cigarettes, and

Baseball purists cringed as Maris
pursued The Babe's immortal record
by walloping them out.

he avoided the press and most interviews. His hair began to fall out, first in trickles, then in clumps.

The pressure increased when Mantle, with 54 home runs, was forced from the lineup for the season with injuries, leaving Maris alone in the spotlight. In the 154th game of the season Roger had 58 home runs, and perhaps he feared hitting more, because he asked manager Ralph Houk that day if he could bunt at the plate instead of swing. Fortunately he reconsidered and slugged number 59 to clinch the pennant for the Yankees. With five games left in the season he hit number 60 to tie Ruth. The next three days his bat was silent, but the fans weren't. Some wanted him to break the record and some didn't, but it seemed everybody had an opinion.

Claire Ruth, the Babe's widow, was in attendance for the season's final game at Yankee Stadium, and she agreed with Frick that it was too late for Maris to beat her husband because 154 games had already been played. Maris flied out his first time up. In his next at bat, he worked Red Sox rookie Tracy Stallard to a 2-0 count. Yankees broadcaster Phil

21

Team:
New York Yankees

Player #:
9

Lifetime Batting Average:
.260

# of HRs (1961):
61

Lefty / Righty:
Left

Positions Played:
Right, Left Field

Maris

Rizzuto made the call: "Here's the wind-up … fastball hit deep to right … this could be it! … way back there! … Holy Cow, he did it! Sixty-one home runs!" As Maris crossed the plate for the record and arrived at his dugout to hide, his teammates would not let him in until he waved to the mostly cheering crowd. When he did they roared.

The record was like a curse for Maris. The next year he had 33 homers and 100 runs batted in, an excellent season by any standard, yet the Associated Press dubbed him "Flop of the Year." He played six more seasons, mostly with a serious hand injury, and quietly retired. Near the end of his life he revealed to a friend that he wished he'd never broken the record. "All it brought me was headaches," he said.

McGwire's childhood nickname
was "Tree," and he has always
stood tall at the plate.

Mighty Mac

It was 13 years after Babe Ruth's death that Roger Maris broke the immortal Babe's record to become the new home run king. Now 13 years after Maris's death another new king was about to be crowned. Mark McGwire believed in fate. He figured 1998 would be his year. It was no coincidence to him that he hit number 61 on his father's 61th birthday. Now, a day later, he stood alone in his St. Louis Cardinals clubhouse and ran his fingers over the bat Maris used to set his record. Then he touched Maris's bat to his heart. Today would be the day, he thought.

Maris hit his record-breaker at his home park. McGwire was home too. Maris hit his in the fourth inning. McGwire came to bat in the fourth. The bases were empty for Maris. The bases were empty now for McGwire. Fate?

Mark grew up in Southern California, and by age 12 he stood six feet tall and was called "Tree" by his friends. He hit tall homers too. "It would look like a pop-up when he first hit it," said Little League teammate Matt Lumsden, "but it would just keep climbing and climbing in the sky and carry over the fence." Mark earned a scholarship to USC, where he broke every school power record, including homers in a season and career. In his first year with the Oakland A's in 1987 he set a major league rookie record with 49 home runs. He and another slugger, Jose Canseco, were known as "The Bash Brothers" as they blasted the A's to three straight World Series. By 1996 McGwire had become a 6-foot, 5-inch, 250-pound ox as he bombed 52 homers, then 58 the following season despite a mid-season trade to the Cardinals.

As McGwire bashed homers in 1998 at a record pace in pursuit of Maris's mark, baseball's league office ordered two detectives to protect him away from the field. More than two weeks still remained in the 1998 season when Mighty Mac reached 61. It wasn't a question of if he would break the

McGwire spends more time waving a pen for kids than he does waving a bat at the plate.

record now but when. As McGwire stepped into the batter's box in the fourth inning with the bases empty, it seemed that all the world was watching. Four of Maris's children were seated in the front row at Busch Stadium holding a framed photograph of their father. Chicago Cubs pitcher Steve Trachsel delivered his first pitch and–boom–McGwire hit a streaking liner to left. The ball cleared the wall in an instant. It was a blast that would echo through time. Fireworks exploded as Big Mac ran crazily around the bases. His 10-year-old son Matthew, the team's batboy, greeted him at home plate, and Mark hoisted Matthew skyward amid the roars. He climbed into the stands to share some words with Maris's children, then saluted the cheering crowd.

McGwire grew so mentally exhausted in the weeks leading up to the heroic moment that it would have surprised no one if he went hitless the final two weeks of the season. Instead, Mighty Mac slugged eight more homers to finish with 70. Seventy! It was an amazing accomplishment by a gentle giant who quietly donates $1 million a year to abused children and

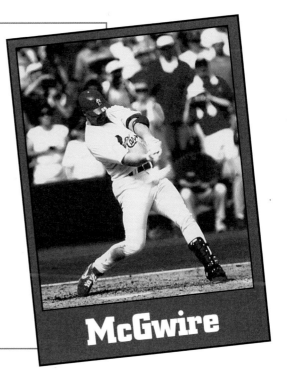

Team:
St. Louis Cardinals

Player #:
25

Lifetime Batting Average:
.264

# of HRs (1998):
70

Lefty / Righty:
Right

Positions Played:
First Base

McGwire

gives away his trophies and awards. McGwire cares little about personal records, but he is the first to admit it would have been unusual to break the home run record yet not even lead the league in home runs that year. How could it happen? Because Mark was not alone in 1998 in his pursuit of history.

Slammin' Sammy

When Mark McGwire drilled his 62nd home run over the left field wall in St. Louis, Sammy Sosa stood in right field and applauded for a moment, then raced in to congratulate Big Mac. Upon seeing Sosa, Mighty Mac threw his arms around the Chicago Cubs outfielder and lifted him into the air. Why did these two opponents care so much about each other? Because the 1998 season had become known as the Great Home Run Race between McGwire and Sosa. When Mac hit his record-breaker, Sosa was right behind with 58. The way Sosa had it figured, McGwire may have reached the summit first, but there were still more than two weeks left in the season, still plenty of games to hit home runs. Sammy congratulated Mark and then told him not to get too far ahead. Maybe Mark listened. Because a few days later Sammy caught McGwire … and then passed him.

30

Although McGwire hit four more homers than Sosa, Sosa was named Most Valuable Player of the year.

Sammy grew up in the Dominican Republic, an island country about 700 miles southeast of the United States and about half the size of the state of Indiana. Sammy lived in the poor town of San Pedro de Macoris where his father died when he was seven years old. He had to earn money to help support his family by washing cars, shining shoes, and selling oranges in the street. Baseball is a popular game among Dominicans, and Sammy became such a good hitter as a youth that a scout for the Texas Rangers spotted him and signed him to their farm system at age 16.

In the middle of Sammy's rookie season with the Rangers in 1989 he was traded to the Chicago White Sox. He played two full seasons with the Sox, hitting 25 homers total, before being traded to the Cubs. He hit eight home runs in his first year with the Cubs, then averaged 30 over his next three seasons. He was criticized for being undisciplined at the plate, swinging at too many bad pitches, and striking out too often. He blasted 40 homers in 1996 and 36 more in 1997, great numbers for most, but not for Sammy, who changed his swing before the 1998 season by learning to keep his weight back. As a reminder he tapped his front foot as the pitcher started his windup. Nobody noticed the change at first, and it didn't seem to help him much. In late May, McGwire had 24 home runs and Sammy had just nine. Then, whoosh, the ball started jumping off his bat. In June he hit 20 home runs. Twenty! Nobody in baseball history had ever hit that many in a month, and suddenly the race was on.

One thing Sosa didn't change was his home run celebration. It consisted of two parts—the hop and the thump-kiss. As soon as the ball left his bat, he would jump in the air in glee and then start his home run trot. That was the hop. After crossing the plate he would thump his heart with his fist and then kiss his fingers in honor of his mother. That was the thump-kiss. Sammy was having fun.

Five days after Sosa watched McGwire hit number 62, he made his own history. On a spectacular late-summer after-noon in Chicago he blasted two homers—numbers 61 and

Team:
Chicago Cubs

Player #:
21

Lifetime Batting Average:
.264

# of HRs (1998):
66

Lefty / Righty:
Right

Positions Played:
Left, Center Field

SOSA

62–to catch Big Mac. He high-fived his teammates, then sat down in the dugout and cried as fans chanted "Sam-my! Sam-my!" He could hardly believe it. A mark that had stood for 37 years had amazingly been passed twice in less than a week. Back in San Pedro de Macoris, residents watching the game on television flooded the streets to celebrate.

Then the race got even more frantic. McGwire hit number 63. Sammy hit number 63. McGwire hit numbers 64 and 65. Sammy hit two in one game to tie Big Mac at 65. Then with three days left in the season, Sammy hit number 66 at the Astrodome in Houston. Fifty-one thousand fans roared as he touched the plate and waved. Suddenly he was ahead of McGwire.

Sammy's lead did not last long. Less than an hour later, McGwire hit his 66th. Then, incredibly, Mighty Mac hit two more Saturday and two more Sunday to finish with 70, leaving Sammy alone in second place all-time with 66. But before you feel bad for Sammy, know that his last regular season game was a victory that pushed his Cubs into the playoffs. Sammy had played 1,247 major league games, and not one of them had been a playoff game–but now that sad streak was over. His team did not reach the World Series in 1998, but he did get to throw out the first ball for Game 1 at Yankee Stadium and enjoy a wonderful parade down the streets of New York City in his honor.

Kings and Kongs

It is said that records are meant to be broken. If so, Babe Ruth wouldn't have minded seeing what happened at 9:07 p.m. on April 8, 1974, at Atlanta Stadium. That was the moment The Babe's career home run record of 714 was eclipsed by Hank Aaron.

Hank's first home run in minor leagues didn't count when he forgot to touch first base and was called out on appeal. From then on, he always looked down at the bases and never watched the ball clear the fence. He missed plenty of excitement. In 23 major league seasons with the Milwaukee (and then Atlanta) Braves and Milwaukee Brewers he smacked 755 homers. His most famous was number 715, which came in front of the Braves' largest crowd ever off Los Angeles Dodgers pitcher Al Downing. Broadcaster Milo Hamilton announced it on television this way: "Here's the

pitch by Downing … Swinging …
There's a drive into left center field.
That ball is gonna beeeeeee …
Outta here! It's 715! There's a new
home run champion of all time and
it's Henry Aaron!" The famous ball
landed in the Braves bullpen where
a teammate retrieved it and returned
it to Hank. Singer Sammy Davis, Jr.
offered $25,000 for it. Hank declined
and today he keeps the ball in a
bank vault.

**Hammerin' Hank is baseball's
all-time home run king.**

Right behind Hammerin' Hank and The Babe on the all-time
list is Willie Mays, also known as "The Say Hey Kid." Willie
hit a home run on his first hit in the major leagues in 1951
and never stopped on his way to 660 total. He would have
had more if he hadn't missed two years serving in the U.S.
Army and spent so much time working on his outfield skills.
He's best known for his World Series catch in 1954 for the

New York Giants in which he caught a ball over his head in center field running full speed with his back to home plate.

Reggie Jackson is Mr. October for his playoff bombs.

Willie moved west with the Giants to thrill San Francisco fans by blasting more bombs before finishing his career back in New York with the Mets.

Trailing Aaron, Ruth, and Mays are sluggers like Frank Robinson (who hit 586 career homers), Harmon Killebrew (573), Reggie Jackson (563), Mike Schmidt (548), Mickey Mantle (536), Jimmie Foxx (534), and Ted Williams and Willie McCovey (521 each). These top 10 sluggers combined for 6,511 home runs. But none was as sudden and dramatic as the greatest single-game blasts. Because just as baseball has its big kings, it has its big kongs—game-winning kongs, that is.

In 1951, Bobby Thomson hit "The Shot Heard Round the World." Few televisions were in homes yet so people gathered in front of appliance store windows to watch the deciding playoff game between New York's National League rival Giants and Dodgers. The Giants trailed 4-1 in the bottom of the ninth when they scratched out a run and put two more runners on. Then Thomson hit the most famous blast of the decade as Giants announcer Russ Hodges made this memorable call: "It's gonna be … I believe … The Giants win the pennant … the Giants win the pennant! … The Giants win the pennant! The Giants win the pennant! Bobby Thomson hits into the lower deck of the left field stands! The Giants win the pennant! I don't believe it!"

Bobby Thomson blasted the Giants to a pennant.

Few believed the ending of the 1960 World Series either. The powerful Yankees had scored more than twice as many

Bill Mazeroski's homer made him a hero for life.

runs combined as the Pittsburgh Pirates in the first six games, but somehow the Pirates had forced a seventh game. The Yanks led 7-4 in the eighth inning and appeared headed for the title, but the Pirates rallied to forge a tie. In the bottom of the ninth inning, slick-fielding second baseman Bill Mazeroski stepped to the plate. No World Series had ever ended with a home run. This one did. Mazeroski hit a blast that carried over left fielder Yogi Berra and the wall. Mazeroski was a hero for life.

Thirty-three years later, in 1993, another World Series ended with a dramatic home run. This time it happened in Toronto. Philadelphia Phillies reliever Mitch "Wild Thing" Williams was struggling to throw strikes in the bottom of the ninth inning against the Blue Jays. His pitches sailed everywhere but over the plate. Wild Thing finally managed to throw a fastball straight down the middle. Joe Carter was ready for it. Carter smashed a drive deep to left and out, and SkyDome erupted in fireworks.

There are other players who will forever be remembered for hitting dramatic World Series homers. Catcher Carlton Fisk hit a blast down the left field line and over the high wall known as the Green Monster at Boston's Fenway Park to give his Red Sox a thrilling 11th inning victory in Game 6 of the 1975 fall classic. The image of Fisk waving his arms for the ball to stay fair are

Carlton Fisk waved a bomb over the Green Monster.

still shown on television. Two years later, in 1977, slugger Reggie Jackson homered in his last at bat of Game 5 for the Yankees, then in Game 6 hit three home runs on three consecutive pitches. For this Jackson became known as Mr.

Kirk Gibson injured the A's with his miracle blast.

October, because that is the month when the World Series is played. In 1989, Kirk Gibson limped to the plate with two outs in the bottom of the ninth with a runner aboard and his Los Angeles Dodgers trailing the Oakland A's by a run. Gibson's legs ached so terribly that he wasn't in the regular lineup, but with the game on the line, he asked to pinch hit. Gibson reached a full count, then fouled off several pitches, wincing in pain each time. Then in a moment hard to believe he lifted a fly ball to right field that carried into the seats. The favored A's never recovered from the shock and lost the Series in five games.

Home Run Facts

*S*ome home runs are long forgotten while others are remembered forever. But all of them are accounted for by baseball historians who compile endless lists of trivia. Here are some of our favorite home run fun facts.

The Most

Twelve players have hit four home runs in one game. They are Bobby Lowe (1894), Ed Delahanty (1896), Lou Gehrig (1932), Chuck Klein (1936), Pat Seerey (1948), Gil Hodges (1950), Joe Adcock (1954), Rocky Colavito (1959), Willie Mays (1961), Mike Schmidt (1976), Bob Horner (1986), and Mark Whiten (1993). Gehrig almost had five, but that ball was caught above the fence.

In 1987 the Toronto Blue Jays hit 10 home runs in one game against the Orioles. The Jays won the game, 18-3.

In 1996 the Baltimore Orioles hit 257 homers to break the single-season mark held by the 1961 New York Yankees.

The Least

Only 39 home runs were hit in the National League's first season in 1876. George Hall led the league with five. He hit two in the same game, the first ever to do it.

The third-place 1908 White Sox hit only three home runs the entire season.

The 1945 Washington Senators hit only one home run all season. It was an inside-the-park job.

Chasing the Babe

Jimmy Foxx hit 58 home runs for the A's in 1932, and he might have broken the record if he hadn't injured his hand falling off a stepladder late in the season.

Hank Greenberg had 58 home runs for the Tigers with five games left in the 1938 season. But the final series, which was scheduled for tiny League Park in Cleveland, was moved to huge Municipal Stadium to accommodate fans wanting to see Greenberg. He hit two long doubles to a fence 460 feet away and finished at 58.

Hack Wilson of the Chicago Cubs hit 56 homers for the Chicago Cubs in 1930. This remained the National League record until 1998 when Mark McGwire and Sammy Sosa both broke it.

Streaks

In 1987 the first three Padres to come to the plate—Marvell Wynn, Tony Gwynn, and John Kruk—homered. The Padres still lost the game.

In 1993 Ken Griffey, Jr. homered in eight straight games for the Seattle Mariners, tying the Major League record held by Dale Long (1956) and Don Mattingly (1987).

In 1996 Andruw Jones of the Atlanta Braves became only the second player ever to hit home runs in his first two World Series at bats. Gene Tenace of the Oakland A's was the first in 1972.

Oddities

In some 19th century ballparks, home runs were only counted if they were hit between outfielders in the field of play, not over their head and into the stands.

Ken Griffey, Jr. could become the all-time home run king.

John Miller homered in the first at bat of his career in 1966. Three years later he homered in the last at bat of his career. He hit none in between.

Jimmy Piersall hit his 100th home run in 1963 and celebrated by circling the bases backward. A rule was made afterward that players must run forward. Piersall was cut from the New York Mets soon after.

The distance of Hank Aaron's home runs strung together stretches halfway from New York to Philadelphia.

The Longest

Babe Ruth hit a shot in 1919 that flew an estimated 587 feet and another in 1926 that went 626 feet.

Harry Heilmann hit one in 1926 that traveled an estimated 660 feet.

Mickey Mantle hit one in 1953 that was actually measured at 565 feet. He hit another in 1960 that was estimated at 643 feet.

Reggie Jackson hit one at the 1969 All-Star Game that was figured at 600 feet.

George Foster mashed a ball in 1977 that flight engineers estimated at 720 feet.

Jose Canseco hit one in 1990 that landed in the fifth deck of Toronto's SkyDome, 600 feet from home plate.

Catcher Ernie Lombardi hit the longest home run by far. He knocked one over the center field fence that landed in a truck, which then drove the ball 30 miles away.

When major league baseball reached the end of the 20th century, nearly a quarter of a million home runs had been hit. Some were among the most famous moments ever in all of sports. How many more will be hit in your lifetime? How many will you see? As long as there are fences in the outfield, and as long as pitchers do their part, you should see plenty of heroes and history. Who knows? Someday you might even be a home run king.

Index